"Elementary Thoughts"

notes written to me from the hearts of children

Written By:

Mindi Lampert, MS, LMHC

authorHOUSE®

AuthorHouse™
1663 Liberty Drive
Bloomington, IN 47403
www.authorhouse.com
Phone: 1 (800) 839-8640

Published by AuthorHouse   12/14/2015

ISBN: 978-1-5049-1974-6 (sc)
ISBN: 978-1-5049-1975-3 (hc)
ISBN: 978-1-5049-1973-9 (e)

Library of Congress Control Number: 2015910429

Print information available on the last page.

Dedication

This book is dedicated to the more than ten thousand children I have counseled over the years. You will forever have a warm and special place in my heart for sharing your "Elementary Thoughts" with me. I will lovingly remember you, always.

It is with my humbled gratitude that these children trusted our bond and felt comfortable and safe enough to disclose their feelings and share their problems with me, in the hope that I was able to lessen their burdens and provide therapeutic comfort.

I also dedicate this book to my loving husband, Elliott, and our children, Jeff and Shirley, Justin and Diana, Joey and Anastasia and our sweet granddaughter, Lily. I have immense love in my heart for each of you, and my personal promise that I will always make myself available for you, when I am needed.

I would like to give a special thank you to my brother Frank Jacobs, who, when I told him my book concept over 15 years ago, came up with this perfect book title.

Introduction

This book is written for parents. It is meant to be a tool of parental enlightenment and awareness into a child's thoughts, insights, pressures and fears. This is also a valuable resource book for Educators.

There are many books on parenting. Books that will tell you "do this" or "don't do that". This is a different kind of parenting book. I wanted to bring you the voice of the children.

I believe this book is most unique and the only book of its kind.

My name is Mindi Lampert. I am a Licensed Mental Health Counselor with a Master of Science degree in Counseling. For the past 18 years, I have been counseling children in Miami Dade County Public Schools; I am a Psychotherapist with a Private Practice for Adults, Adolescents and Children, a Florida Supreme Court Certified Family Mediator and am an Adjunct Professor at Miami Dade College where I teach classes in Psychology and Student Life Skills.

Children come to school every day with their family baggage. Some are angry, mad, and sad. They feel lonely and isolated. Some feel unloved, unattached, neglected, completely ignored or forgotten. In the morning, with sadness, I have watched as mothers and fathers drop their children off at school and am amazed at how many parents are busy chatting on their cell phones while their kids are in the backseat looking around for some connection. The kids are not getting what they want and need most, their parent's attention. This is what they most desire. This is indeed a missed opportunity for parents. Sometimes those disconnected children behave badly at school, misbehave or even take their anger out of other kids, anything for attention. After all negative attention, although negative, is still attention. Then, once the principal calls their parents to come to school for misbehavior, now they have their parents attention.

Children very often will hide their feelings from their parents. They do this for different reasons. Sometimes, they think their parents will be mad, sometimes they think their parents will be sad and they are trying to protect their parents from getting hurt. This is very common in cases of separation and divorce.

My job is to let children know that they have a safe and private place to talk about their problems and feelings; the issues that are aching in their hearts and heavy of their minds. After all, how can they be expected to perform at their academic best if they're feeling overwhelmed—they cannot. They need to share their thoughts, their *"Elementary Thoughts."* They need to organize their thinking and disclose their feelings into a positive direction. Listening is the key.

Whatever the issue or crisis is I always let children know that they need self-empowerment and positive thinking to conquer life's negative situations, the many bumpy roads of life...

Children have many challenges. The number one, most often, theme troubling the children that come to see me relates to family issues— *i.e.* parents fighting, separation and divorce—and how they are trying to come to terms with the inequality of the family systems. There are also a surprising number of children who experience great sadness.

When a child requests counseling with me, they handwrite a note. The notes are evidence of the child's raw emotions, pain, innocence and vulnerability. This book is a compilation of over 400 notes that elementary aged children, ages 6 – 11 years old have written to me. The notes are divided into 19 different life issues that span more than a decade of research and collection. I have only identified the note by the sex of the child, B for Boy, G for Girl and their grade level, K – 5 for anonymity, no names are on the notes.

The notes are in the children's handwriting. The notes portray the essence of their innocence; along with all their grammar and spelling errors that make the notes that much more endearing and should truly reach your heart. Some notes that were written in crayon had to be traced over to be able to be read by you.

Your challenge is to read them. I am sure you will be surprised by much of what you read. The notes have not only touched me but, have on many occasions, broken my heart by the magnitude of the heaviness that some children carry in their heart.

"If parents only knew what their kids were thinking" was my mantra, so I wrote this book for you.

3

Notes by Life Issues / Chapters

Chapter 1

Sadness

I love my mom very much but for some reason everytime me or my brother disobey her or do bad things a rain of sadness just like falls on me & I start crying for no reason at all & want to stop. 3/G

Student Request For Counseling
with Mrs. Lampert

May I Please Talk To You About...

How I've been and how I cant find anything good about myself 5/E

I feel like I do not be long here at all. No one likes to play with me at all. All the boy are bullying me. Every day and I do not like that. But not all the boys. When we are in line they think that I am trying to go in front of them. I wish that will stop. Help me I very sad.   3/G

Student Request For Counseling
with Mrs. Lampert

May I Please Talk To You About....

a lot of peple are lafing to me.   4/G

Student Request For Counseling
with Mrs. Lampert

May I Please Talk To You About...

I keep on crying cause miss my my mom   4/G

Student Request For Counseling
with Mrs. Lampert

May I Please Talk To You About…

My Mom is sad a lot
and when she sad I cry. 5/G

Student Request For Counseling
with Mrs. Lampert

May I Please Talk To You About…

People always makes me be 3/B
sad and agry when they
always cull me litte they make fun of me.

Student Request For Counseling
with Mrs. Lampert

May I Please Talk To You About…

me with school and I'm… Just so
depressed 4/B

Student Request For Counseling
with Mrs. Lampert

May I Please Talk To You About…

What People think about my talents and Dreams They always say I cant do it 3/G

Student Request For Counseling
with Mrs. Lampert

May I Please Talk To You About…

I am feeling a little down every day. 3/G

May I Please Talk To You About…

Family problem I cry always need help! 5/G

Student Request For Counseling
with Mrs. Lampert

May I Please Talk To You About…

How Some times I alwasy feel
Sad Just for ~~things~~ Small things.

3/G

(stutter)
I have a problem because I Started.
a lot and a lot of People is laughing.
at me and copying me a lot and
That make me Sad. I am neRvous a
lot to talk out loud and I don't
like to read out loud in front
of People.

Please Help me.

4/G

I need Help because I come +
cry every day (family)

5/G

10

Student Request For Counseling
with Mrs. Lampert

May I Please Talk To You About...

My Sadness in School and
I've been dipressed   3/G

Student Request For Counseling
with Mrs. Lampert

May I Please Talk To You About...

People who alway make fun of my
age, size, and grade, and I'm tired of   3/B
them doing that.

Student Request For Counseling
with Mrs. Lampert

May I Please Talk To You About...   2/B

I am feeling sad
about my grand father.

Student Request For Counseling
with Mrs. Lampert

May I Please Talk To You About…

~~because~~ every time people tell secrets to other
people infront of me I feel sad. I told my
mom but she doesn't seem to understand me. wat do I do?
4/G

Student Request For Counseling
with Mrs. Lampert

May I Please Talk To You About…

The class Im in. Everyone is beeing a
jeerk and I dont now why. Im
really lonely
4/G

STUDENT REQUEST FOR COUNSELING

MAY I PLEASE TALK TO YOU ABOUT… 4/B

feeling sad

Draw a picture of how you feel inside. 3/B

A Time When I Felt

When I'm allway's sad
it's for a reson and the
reason is because of
how people treat me how
they talk to me and it's
not fair but I have happy
times in my life with my famil,

5/G

Imagine that you go to see a fortune teller. Draw a picture or tell
about what your future will look like.

I think my future will be sad, not happy, i cry ing, mad, i be a sad teacher and like to be alone. Then I have no friend or noth- ing but my safe. and I don't fell safe. I racher, be like this

4/G

The reson that I am sad is
because somtimes my mom and
dad fight somtime I dont feel
like doing antling and its sorery
and because I think thet am
the onley one that doesent
talk to there mom you now
like haveing a real conversason.
That is way am sad.

4/G

Student Request For Counseling
with Mrs. Lampert

May I Please Talk To You About…

bad feeling i get.

4/G

My sister ows a lot of money. And
my mom keeps crying and crying a bout
and it is making me verey sad.

3/G

16

STUDENT REQUEST FOR COUNSELING

MAY I PLEASE TALK TO YOU ABOUT...

I'm feeling useless
and unwanted by anybody   4/G

"

Student Request For Counseling
with Mrs. Lampert

May I Please Talk To You About...

Family problem and I'm really
sad
                              5/G

It was a time when I felt sad that
My sister was fighting with my mom
and my sister moved out of the
house I was Crying for 4 days
then on the weekend I saw her
in my dads house.

4/B

Student Request For Counseling
with Mrs. Lampert

May I Please Talk To You About…

That Dad is in the hos petal
and very sad .   3/G

My grand mother is very sick as is my
sister my mother crys for hours and my
grand mother is in the hostaple she
was a dog a preshes dog my dog killed
it by one bite the blood was every
were I have night mares now I cant
tell my gran mother I have ben
living with it for a month I cant
stand it!

3/G

STUDENT REQUEST FOR COUNSELING

MAY I PLEASE TALK TO YOU ABOUT…

I have do the note all roody
and I bine talking about my father
My Mom .   4/G

Sometimes I feel like killing myself because not a person notice me, don't care about me. But you almost seem you care about me. But don't try to stop me for saying this I don't know why this to happen to me but one thing I know I'm still going to have anger in me. Not one can stop my anger. But God trust helps a little but not much so thanks to mics. Lampet for trying to help me out but it's not going to work this time but not at all But a little

So thanks for trying Mrs. Lampet

4/G

Dear, ███████ I'm not
having a good ████ ██
Day Because of
I Just know if ███████
Dont leave me alone Something
is going to happen. Also
last week my Dad
gave me a letter saying
That it was a mostake
For me to Be Born He
raped my mom when
she had me so now
I never want to talk to
him agin When I found
out I was
so shoked and sad
But I need to leave That
Behined and forget That.
and Just Be glad I have
parents

4/G

What Happened? ~~I at it~~ am ~~wor~~ I am sad because I let go of my best friend ▮▮▮▮ and I will never see him again. My mom and Dad are in a ~~▮▮~~ devorce so we have only a little bit of money. But I am mostly lonely.

4/B

Chapter 2

Peer Issues / Bullying

Student Request For Counseling
with Mrs. Lampert

May I Please Talk To You About…

My Class because they are all being mean and making fun of Me. 5/B

Student Request For Counseling
with Mrs. Lampert

May I Please Talk To You About…

I feel left out by my friends 5/G

Ms. lampert a boy named
Lie every time and he made me made me feel bad. said I

3G

_____ is Bieng
A bully and I'm trying
to Fitt in whith my
Freinds and he is
Sauing in anberusing
things a bout me
and he won't stop
can you help Me? 4/

Student Request For Counseling
with Mrs. Lampert

May I Please Talk To You About... 3/G

Eury time I turn around
I feel like people are laughing
that at only girl and saving woh look ot who it is

I need Help Because
kid's keep on Doing many thing's to me
that make me Feel like I am a 5/G
nodody

Mrs. Lampert

Dear miss Lampert
please help me everyone
keeps on making fun of me
and if i cry they will call
me a baby please help
4/G

Student Request For Counseling
with Mrs. Lampert

May I Please Talk To You About...

I feel like some people are laughing at 3/G
me behind my back.

Student Request For Counseling
with Mrs. Lampert

May I Please Talk To You About...

3/G

My problems with how ███████
treats me and insults me. It hearts me.

Student Request For Counseling
with Mrs. Lampert

May I Please Talk To You About...

3/G

I feel like I am chubby. I know
you said that none of us are chubby & th
at you hate it when little kids think tha
→
←

they are chubby but I really feel like
it. I also feel like I don't fit in because of my chubbyness. Like I see all my
Friends & they are skinny but I'm not
Please talk to me about it.

Student Request For Counseling
with Mrs. Lampert

May I Please Talk To You About…

~~ckt~~ every Body keeps on
calling me names and fat it   4/G
Makes me feel Bad I cry.

Student Request For Counseling
with Mrs. Lampert

May I Please Talk To You About…

a Kid bulling in my class   5/8

People always call me that
Im over weight and I say
Im Proud of it. But it still
Dosent work for My feelings.
                          4/G

STUDENT REQUEST FOR COUNSELING

MAY I PLEASE TALK TO YOU ABOUT...

My Friend that's always teasing me
about every thing please call me.   5/G

STUDENT REQUEST FOR COUNSELING

MAY I PLEASE TALK TO YOU ABOUT...

the people in my class are
being mean to me now this is   4/G
serious please let me talk to you abou

I want to talk about
kids Piking at me and
calling me foureyes.   3/G

Student Request For Counseling
with Mrs. Lampert

May I Please Talk To You About…

I feel like No one Needs My help and they all wish i was 100 Years old so I be dead   3/B

Student Request For Counseling
with Mrs. Lampert

May I Please Talk To You About…

The are some kids are bothering us and teasing us   3/B

Student Request For Counseling
with Mrs. Lampert

May I Please Talk To You About…

Someone is messing with me.   4/B

Student Request For Counseling
with Mrs. Lampert

May I Please Talk To You About…

Bullging saying his going to brake my
face and pop my eyes   3/8

Student Request For Counseling
with Mrs. Lampert

May I Please Talk To You About…

This boy in our class is
talking bad things about 5/6
me to my friends

Student Request For Counseling
with Mrs. Lampert

May I Please Talk To You About…

I have a girlfriend and I keep
On having mixed feeling   5/8

Student Request For Counseling
with Mrs. Lampert

May I Please Talk To You About… Can you help me
miss Lampert

that my friend doesn't want to
be my friend any more. I think
its because shes has two new friends. I feel leftout

5/G

Student Request For Counseling
with Mrs. Lampert

May I Please Talk To You About…

Some one is saing gosip to
Other people about me.

3/B

Student Request For Counseling
with Mrs. Lampert

May I Please Talk To You About…

Dear mrs lamper I want to talk about
when I don't like when People say that
I have a big had.

3/G

Dear Ms. lampert   from: ████████

ok this is #3 of notes
I send you but this is
the worst this kid (████████)
keeps pushing me around
the worst part he is in
my Class (ms ████ class) also   4/8
he keeps pushing me
literaly!

Student Request For Counseling
with Mrs. Lampert

May I Please Talk To You About...

My friends are not talking
to me, but am to scared to tell   4/6
them Something. What do I do?

Student Request For Counseling
with Mrs. Lampert

May I Please Talk To You About...

My classmate is bothering
me and being mean.   4/6
to me. I can take it any moe

Student Request For Counseling
with Mrs. Lampert

May I Please Talk To You About...

MY friend is not himself.

4/B

People telling me that I'm to small to do anything

4/G

Student Request For Counseling
with Mrs. Lampert

May I Please Talk To You About...

people are making fun
of me

5/B

Student Request For Counseling
with Mrs. Lampert

May I Please Talk To You About…

There is this girl that keeps on making fun of me and she talks bad about me. 3/G

Student Request For Counseling
with Mrs. Lampert

May I Please Talk To You About…

To tell a person to stop Making fun of me she's been makeing fun of me since the beginning. 5/B

Student Request For Counseling
with Mrs. Lampert

May I Please Talk To You About…

People keep on calling me fat. 3/B

Student Request For Counseling
with Mrs. Lampert

May I Please Talk To You About…

Me always getting named

called. . 3/B

Student Request For Counseling
with Mrs. Lampert

May I Please Talk To You About…

A girl that keeps on telling me what to 3/G
do and a boy never knows what to do for
homework and he asks me how to do it when I am working.

Student Request For Counseling
with Mrs. Lampert

May I Please Talk To You About…

This girl that I said if she 3/G
did pea in her pants and she
words. is know cursing me with really bar

Student Request For Counseling
with Mrs. Lampert

May I Please Talk To You About…

About my frieds that
are mean to me   . 4/B

Student Request For Counseling
with Mrs. Lampert

May I Please Talk To You About…

My friend ████ & I keep arguing   . 4/G

STUDENT REQUEST FOR COUNSELING

MAY I PLEASE TALK TO YOU ABOUT…

abat somebody I like
By he does not like me   5/G

Student Request For Counseling
with Mrs. Lampert

May I Please Talk To You About…

A Box That Keeps calling me
Stupid and Dome and hes
Making me mad.   4/8

Student Request For Counseling
with Mrs. Lampert

May I Please Talk To You About…

MY Freinds they keep saying
That I'm stupid.   4/8

Student Request For Counseling
with Mrs. Lampert

May I Please Talk To You About…

a girl who keeps calling
me names and saxs I   4/8
stupid.

Student Request For Counseling
with Mrs. Lampert

May I Please Talk To You About...

Personal facts about girls.

5/G

Student Request For Counseling
with Mrs. Lampert

May I Please Talk To You About...

This Kid Keeed on saying I am short and it hurts my feelings.

5/B

Student Request For Counseling
with Mrs. Lampert

May I Please Talk To You About...

███████ heeps Calling me fatty and he called me a fatt suma wrester

3/G

People keep writing
about me and they
don't like me they
hate me ▇▇▇▇ I only have
1 friend ▇▇▇▇▇▇
No 1 else they also
talk about me Please
help me no one wants
to say some thing
about me they also
talk about me in secret
that I'm ugly and fat
they also call ▇▇▇▇
that talking about my
family help me 3/G please

Student Request For Counseling
with Mrs. Lampert

May I Please Talk To You About...

I feel like my Life is falling apart because
▇▇▇▇▇▇▇ all of my friends are
acting weird & I have no Idea why   5/G

Student Request For Counseling
with Mrs. Lampert

May I Please Talk To You About…

███ ~~≋~~ She always wants
to be Prerty For all Boys
And wants to be Frist She is
3/G
like
i'm
So
Cute

Student Request For Counseling
with Mrs. Lampert

May I Please Talk To You About…

Girls in my class Bugging me
and making Fun of me. 5/G

Student Request For Counseling
with Mrs. Lampert

May I Please Talk To You About…

Friends and gossip, 5/G

Student Request For Counseling
with Mrs. Lampert

May I Please Talk To You About…

I told my DaD about the preer presure.   5/B

Student Request For Counseling
with Mrs. Lampert

May I Please Talk To You About…

With Ferred's saying they don't like me and they don't want to be my Friend's   4/G

Student Request For Counseling
with Mrs. Lampert

May I Please Talk To You About…

My friend wont talk to me I feel invisible I feel leftout Can you help me with my problem?   5/G

Student Request For Counseling
with Mrs. Lampert

May I Please Talk To You About…

Kids are picking on me and They are pushing me and hurting my feelings ——— 3/G

Student Request For Counseling
with Mrs. Lampert

May I Please Talk To You About…

Everone think that I'm a'm weird and boring. 4/G

Nobody talk to me in school whats wrong with me? 3/6

Chapter 3

Parents Fighting

Student Request For Counseling
with Mrs. Lampert

May I Please Talk To You About…

my mom and dad are starting to fight 4/G
agian but not as much as before but
they get a little loud and I get scared

Mrs
lampert
It is not
working
they are still
Fighting 3/G

Student Request For Counseling
with Mrs. Lampert

May I Please Talk To You About…

My parents started getting along but know 4/G
they fight for dumb reasons but they always

Student Request For Counseling
with Mrs. Lampert

May I Please Talk To You About...

My mom and dad always fight and when ~~[scribbled out]~~ Their mad they take there feelings out on me and always scream at me   5/G

Dear, Miss Lampert My parents are fighting I do not know what to do. There mean too each other ⚘   3/G

Student Request For Counseling
with Mrs. Lampert

May I Please Talk To You About...

My parent's fight a lot & I can't stand it anymore.

— B/4th

Student Request For Counseling
with Mrs. Lampert

May I Please Talk To You About...

My Mom and dad have Been figting and I usally Get very Scared.

— G/3rd

Student Request For Counseling
with Mrs. Lampert

May I Please Talk To You About...

aBout my mom and dad there elways having Big Big Big Fights my dad screams ALOT and my mom not so much screams my moms nice, my dad scy hes strickt

B/3rd

STUDENT REQUEST FOR COUNSELING

MAY I PLEASE TALK TO YOU ABOUT...

My mom and my ~~dod~~ dad
fite and ~~my~~ my sister
and my borther criye.   G/5th

I want to talk about thing
that has been going on in my
Family. I think that they
are going to Break up.
they make me mad.
what can you do to
help.
                                    B/4th

STUDENT REQUEST FOR COUNSELING

MAY I PLEASE TALK TO YOU ABOUT...

My parents are fighting more
and I just cant stand it because G/5th
It makes me just want to pick somebee too
                                    live with

48

May I Please Talk To You About…

My Mom and my dad every time I think about my mom and my dad and sometimes I cry or just tell my Dad.   B/3rd

Note

Dear Mrs. lampert

My parents have been going threw a tuff time with the money and there fighting because of that. Also I'm not feeling good because of that.   B/4th

Dear Mrs. lampert

I've had trouble in the past and I have visited you before and my parents keep fighting and they say they have to Devorce as fast as they can and I always get worried,   B/4

May I Please Talk To You About…

My problem is that my parents fight all the time when I come back from my aunts house and I get nervous and I cry alot   4/G

Student Request For Counseling
with Mrs. Lampert

May I Please Talk To You About…

My Dad he his really
Nice but my mom hates
him please i need to talk to
you!

G/3rd

STUDENT REQUEST FOR COUNSELING

MAY I PLEASE TALK TO YOU ABOUT…

I need to talk to you about
my parents Argument when you
have time

G/4th

STUDENT REQUEST FOR COUNSELING

MAY I PLEASE TALK TO YOU ABOUT…

MY MOM had a big
Fight with my step Dad.

G/5th

STUDENT REQUEST FOR COUNSELING

MAY I PLEASE TALK TO YOU ABOUT...

MS. Lampert I want to talk about the war and about My parents fight and about my feelings

G/4th

STUDENT REQUEST FOR COUNSELING

MAY I PLEASE TALK TO YOU ABOUT...

I need to talk to you about my parents with their fighting.

B/5th

My family problem is that my parents are fighting too much and my dad keeps leaving the house for many days. I don't feel good about that. I need to go to TRUST Because I need somebody I can TRUST!

G/4th

Student Request For Counseling
with Mrs. Lampert

May I Please Talk To You About…

that i am sad Because my DaD and my mom
are fighting and my DaD is trying to hurt my   G/3rd
mom and that's why my mom dost Now that i know

STUDENT REQUEST FOR COUNSELING

MAY I PLEASE TALK TO YOU ABOUT…

my Home because My mother
and Step DaD because they keep   6/5th
having fights.

STUDENT REQUEST FOR COUNSELING

MAY I PLEASE TALK TO YOU ABOUT…

Mom anddad fighting
every night
                                    B/5th

Student Request For Counseling
with Mrs. Lampert

May I Please Talk To You About....

My Perents thyre fighting last time teyre were yelling I got nerves and I threw up.

G/3rd

Student Request For Counseling
with Mrs. Lampert

May I Please Talk To You About...

I need to talk with you because my percns are arguing.

B/5th

Student Request For Counseling
with Mrs. Lampert

May I Please Talk To You About...

How I feal about me and my Grandmothers fights and my grandmothers and my grandferthers fights.

G/3rd

Chapter 4

Divorce & Separation

Student Request For Counseling
with Mrs. Lampert

May I Please Talk To You About...

1 My mom is getting Divorced! really Bad!! ② My Bird flew away and I saw him dead at Walmart(!!) 6/4th

Student Request For Counseling
with Mrs. Lampert

May I Please Talk To You About...

My Dad left me my mom and my sister. I can't forget about it. evry day when I m with my Dad and he drops me off. Im alwes crying. 6/3rd

I'm moving but I have to pick my mom or my Dad and I can't take it 6/4th

Student Request For Counseling
with Mrs. Lampert

May I Please Talk To You About… 4/G

My parents ARE makeirg
me go to court Because
~~she~~ they want me to pick who I
~~Name~~ want to be with
~~Teacher~~ more.

beSt

COUNSilor

Student Request For Counseling
with Mrs. Lampert

May I Please Talk To You About…

My parents time out it's been foreverr
ᵇ♂ I am kinda worried.   4/G

Student Request For Counseling
with Mrs. Lampert

May I Please Talk To You About…

I don't under stand why my parents arn't
togethor because they never fight.   4/G

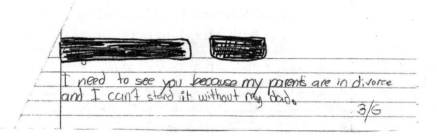

I need to see you because my parents are in divorce
and I can't stand it without my dad.   3/G

my
m om
and my
dad is
devores and
I am so
sad very   3/G
Sad

Dear Dad,
If you didn't come to see me I would be mad at you because you tell me that your coming but you never come. When my mom told me you were coming on Saturday, I got very happy, I think your coming this time. I hope to see you soon.

G/4th

Student Request For Counseling
with Mrs. Lampert

May I Please Talk To You About…

My parents they were going to divorse and they didn't but my mind   G/5th
can't get off it and keep thinking their going to divorse

STUDENT REQUEST FOR COUNSELING

MAY I PLEASE TALK TO YOU ABOUT...

My mom & Dad are getting Devorsed.

Student Request For Counseling
with Mrs. Lampert

May I Please Talk To You About…

My step dad   left my mom and -
me, my brother, my mom are sad and we
are about to lose the house.   G/4th

Student Request For Counseling
with Mrs. Lampert

May I Please Talk To You About…

My Mom   always   says -
she wants   a   divorce   B/5th

My dad is seperated to my
mom and he gave my mom
an in sult.
                                              G/4th

Student Request For Counseling
with Mrs. Lampert

May I Please Talk To You About...

my parents ~~getting dibros~~ getting 6/4th
dibros because they dont andrecrstand .
~~☒ ☒~~ echother so thats way I did to ☒ talk to you
.tank yu

Student Request For Counseling
with Mrs. Lampert

May I Please Talk To You About...   6/5th

I want to keep talking about
the divorce

Student Request For Counseling
with Mrs. Lampert

May I Please Talk To You About...

~~My Dad wants to live with him~~
My Dad wants me to live with him . 6/5th

STUDENT REQUEST FOR COUNSELING

MAY I PLEASE TALK TO YOU ABOUT...

My parents are fighting
and my mom wants
a defores   G/5th

My dad does not let me
se my mom very often and
my mom just came out
of the hospital and I
always miss my mom

B/3rd

Student Request For Counseling
with Mrs. Lampert

May I Please Talk To You About...

Parent Problems : Moving separate
from my mom and Dad.   G/4th

STUDENT REQUEST FOR COUNSELING

MAY I PLEASE TALK TO YOU ABOUT...

My problem is how my family is breaking apart

G/5th

STUDENT REQUEST FOR COUNSELING

MAY I PLEASE TALK TO YOU ABOUT...

Dear Mrs. Lampert I need to talk to you about my mom a dad get devorsted and about my mom, sister and me moving to my grandmas house

G/4th

STUDENT REQUEST FOR COUNSELING

MAY I PLEASE TALK TO YOU ABOUT...

My parent getteing Davorce it's bad.

G/5th

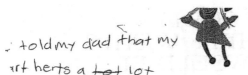

... told my dad that my
art herts a ~~lot~~ lot

Student Request For Counseling
with Mrs. Lampert

May I Please Talk To You About…

~~My~~ ~~parents~~ ~~and~~ and ~~my dad mostly~~
and I want to talk about my dad and
my parents getting divorce   G/4th

Student Request For Counseling
with Mrs. Lampert

May I Please Talk To You About…

My mom and Dad I don't   G/4th
like passing things to person to person
~~they~~ they make me pass things on just
because they don't want to
see each other.

STUDENT REQUEST FOR COUNSELING

MAY I PLEASE TALK TO YOU ABOUT…

Anwser to devorsment!

——————————————————————— B/4th

IF I COULD
HAVE THREE WISHES
THEY WOULD BE:

If I could have Three wishes They would be To see MY dad one MY birthday.

G/3rd

STUDENT REQUEST FOR COUNSELING

MAY I PLEASE TALK TO YOU ABOUT...

my mom & Dad Getting Divorced
B. This is an
Emergency!!!

G/3rd
149

STUDENT REQUEST FOR COUNSELING

Emergency
MAY I PLEASE TALK TO YOU ABOUT...

My chace between leaving with my mom
or leaving with my dad They said that they

G/5th

Student Request For Counseling
with Mrs. Lampert

May I Please Talk To You About...

My parents Just had a divorce
and it hurts alot can you please 6/5th
~~talk to me~~.

Student Request For Counseling
with Mrs. Lampert

May I Please Talk To You About...

is that my aunt got devorce and
I cant concentrate on my work. 8/4th

Student Request For Counseling
with Mrs. Lampert

May I Please Talk To You About...

My step father and my mom are
geting divorced me and my mom
are trying for him to get together again. 6/2rd

Daer Dad

    I miss you when will you come to vist me. will I ever see you. Well all I whanted to tell you is that.You Don't have to live me at my moms house all of the time when you go out. I miss you very much. Can you call me?

6/3rd

Student Request For Counseling
with Mrs. Lampert

May I Please Talk To You About...

My parents My house get lossing my house Divorce My dad coming to the United states

G/5th

Chapter 5

Parents Dating
&
Relationships After Divorce

Student Request For Counseling
with Mrs. Lampert

May I Please Talk To You About…

My dad and his girlfriend she keeps making me in trouble for nothing and she aluagls tells me to get something for her *when shes next to it!*   5/G

May I Please Talk To You About…

That My dad & mom are in a time out and my dad has a girl friend and she has children but I don't like them together.   4/G

my mom got a call frome my step mom matheing fun of her when my mom was sick at the Hospital. my mom and Her Dont get along. I need Help. Shes always mean 2 my mom. ∧ ∧ ∧   4/G

May I Please Talk To You About…

Please help me I have a situation that my mom has a new boy friend and I dont know what to say to him.   5/G

Student Request For Counseling
with Mrs. Lampert

May I Please Talk To You About…

My mom and dad decause my dad did not
come to christmas last year because
he spendid time with his girlfriend. 3/G

Student Request For Counseling
with Mrs. Lampert

May I Please Talk To You About…

My mom dosen't hang out with me she leaves me
by myself all the time she dosen't say she loves me orhug
me, also I'm not happy with the man she married 5/G

May I Please Talk To You About…

■ Dad's at my ~~~~~~~ because every thing that
I always want she get's it for her 5/G
daughter.

STUDENT REQUEST FOR COUNSELING

MAY I PLEASE TALK TO YOU ABOUT...

My Parents because the are not together anymore and my dad is seeing another person and thats all.   G/5th

Student Request For Counseling
with Mrs. Lampert

May I Please Talk To You About...

My dad dating already even though it has only been 1 month.   G/4th

Student Request For Counseling
with Mrs. Lampert

May I Please Talk To You About...

my mom and me not wanting her to date   G/5th

70

Student Request For Counseling
with Mrs. Lampert

May I Please Talk To You About…

everS thing worked out with
Me not wantiing my mom to
date

5/G

Student Request For Counseling
with Mrs. Lampert

May I Please Talk To You About…

That my mom & dad are seperated but
yesterday ████ my dad was with his Gilfriend
my mom doesn't know do I tell her or keep it I'm not good keeping secrets
with my mom

5/G

Mindi Lampert, MS, LMHC

Student Request For Counseling
with Mrs. Lampert

May I Please Talk To You About…

I feel like my dad is thinking to
much about his wife and not about
us..... G/5th

Student Request For Counseling
with Mrs. Lampert

May I Please Talk To You About…

My Dad has go stemp mom
My Dad got mary But I like
Any But his wif she is mean at me   G/3rd

Student Request For Counseling
with Mrs. Lampert

May I Please Talk To You About…

Farther is being mean to me and family
but not going to be wife.

G/4th

Dear Ms. LamPert

Can I have a meeting with you because my mom and Dad haD got a Divorce And my Dad married to another woman And I miss him so can I talk with you B/4th

STUDENT REQUEST FOR COUNSELING

MAY I PLEASE TALK TO YOU ABOUT...

about my mom and
BOY frend and dad   6/3rd

Student Request For Counseling
with Mrs. Lampert

May I Please Talk To You About...

i went to my fathers house &
i feel very happy.   6/4th

Dear ████ group well
I hate to use
the word hate But
My Dad got me mad
When he told me
that he wanted
to see his girlfriend
enstead his kids
But I'm going to try forget about
him Me and my sister
kids are a gift for him all
there is a gift to

74

But Some Parents
Don't know that
Also when My Dad said he
Don't love me that really
realy
Sometimes I feel like My
life is ruen Sometimes
I would like to start
My life over
agin I wish it got
granted.

5/6

Chapter 6

Family Issues

Student Request For Counseling
with Mrs. Lampert

May I Please Talk To You About…

I havent seen my real dad in 7 years and
I really want to see him but I'm
scared to ask her, My mom

5/G

Student Request For Counseling
with Mrs. Lampert

May I Please Talk To You About…

my dad he is being really mean and
he left my family.

5/G

May I Please Talk To You About…

3/G

I'm sorry to bother you
but it's once again about
my Father. Thank you for your time

77

Student Request For Counseling
with Mrs. Lampert

May I Please Talk To You About…

My mom takes advantage of me and my grandma
She always thinks that if she say's it you
just have to do it

4/G

Student Request For Counseling
with Mrs. Lampert

May I Please Talk To You About…

My mom always pushes me to the baby and
Im always with him I mean I love him
but to have all the time is kind of anoying

5/G

Student Request For Counseling
with Mrs. Lampert

May I Please Talk To You About…

My mom and sister have
been fighting and it makes
me sad

3/G

Student Request For Counseling
with Mrs. Lampert

May I Please Talk To You About...

My Dad's opration - Surgry / Pain.   3/G

Student Request For Counseling
with Mrs. Lampert

May I Please Talk To You About...

My Dad I don't get to do much with
him I Feel like he's not my dad   3/G
so I would like to talk to you.

Student Request For Counseling
with Mrs. Lampert

May I Please Talk To You About…

My ~~Dad~~ *Dad* always put's me in 2 place he doesnt care about anything that I do and it bothers me.

4/G

Student Request For Counseling
with Mrs. Lampert

May I Please Talk To You About…

My trip was fine but most of it was not. My dad was so and to meen to me. He does not understand me at all.

5/G

I want to talk to you becuase somthing is going on with my family

5/A

Student Request For Counseling
with Mrs. Lampert

May I Please Talk To You About…

My mom dosen't hang out with me she leaves me
by myself all the time. she dosen't say she loves me or hug
me, also I'm not happy with the man she married   4/B

Student Request For Counseling
with Mrs. Lampert

May I Please Talk To You About…

I try to be nice to my dad but he
doesn't want to be nice to me... like this   5/G
morning, call me ~~tomor~~ tomorrow in the morning.

Student Request For Counseling
with Mrs. Lampert

May I Please Talk To You About…

about my mom its like she dosent   4/B
care about me and blames me for everything
and only cares about Herself and no one
els.

STUDENT REQUEST FOR COUNSELING

MAY I PLEASE TALK TO YOU ABOUT...

my mom and my dad are having my
problems

5/G

STUDENT REQUEST FOR COUNSELING

MAY I PLEASE TALK TO YOU ABOUT...

I want to talk to you about my
problems in my family. By myself

4/G

STUDENT REQUEST FOR COUNSELING

MAY I PLEASE TALK TO YOU ABOUT...

My dad its like, I can't talk to him
I don't know whats wrong
with that please call me tomorrow

4/G

STUDENT REQUEST FOR COUNSELING

MAY I PLEASE TALK TO YOU ABOUT...

My PeBc is My MoM
(problem)

2/B

STUDENT REQUEST FOR COUNSELING

MAY I PLEASE TALK TO YOU ABOUT...

My dad Got mad at me and yelled at me becouse a foot ball game and yelled at my mom for nothing. 4/G

STUDENT REQUEST FOR COUNSELING

MAY I PLEASE TALK TO YOU ABOUT...

May I talk about my dad's anger and problems with family. 4/B

STUDENT REQUEST FOR COUNSELING

MAY I PLEASE TALK TO YOU ABOUT...

I need to talk about the problems that happend today with me, my dad, and my mom.

4/G

STUDENT REQUEST FOR COUNSELING

MAY I PLEASE TALK TO YOU ABOUT...

About my family and me with Problems

3/G

STUDENT REQUEST FOR COUNSELING

MAY I PLEASE TALK TO YOU ABOUT...

4/G

I have to tell you about my real dad.

Student Request For Counseling
with Mrs. Lampert

May I Please Talk To You About…

I said mean things to my family;
I hate them & I wanted a new
family o   4/G

STUDENT REQUEST FOR COUNSELING

MAY I PLEASE TALK TO YOU ABOUT…

Can I speak to you about
My Mom really- bad.
                                    4/G

STUDENT REQUEST FOR COUNSELING

MAY I PLEASE TALK TO YOU ABOUT…

I want to talk
about my dad and   3/G
my mom.

Student Request For Counseling
with Mrs. Lampert

May I Please Talk To You About…

A boyt a family problem. that I have a big tning sometimes I get upset can I talk with you. 3/6

Student Request For Counseling
with Mrs. Lampert

May I Please Talk To You About…

how my Dad is treating me 3/B

Student Request For Counseling
with Mrs. Lampert

May I Please Talk To You About…

My mom because she does not have a rob. 3/6

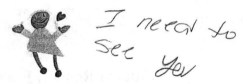

Student Request For Counseling
with Mrs. Lampert

May I Please Talk To You About…

I am having problem at home that
is way I did not come to school
I dont want to move with my dad I am
Leaving this Friday

4/G

Student Request For Counseling
with Mrs. Lampert

May I Please Talk To You About…

My Dad and mom being mad if
I get bad grades but if they want to
spank me

3/G

with Mrs. Lampert

May I Please Talk To You About…

That I lie to my parents, then it makes me
feel bad.

5/G

Student Request For Counseling
with Mrs. Lampert

May I Please Talk To You About…

my dad my mom put me in soccer and I feel
like my dad doesn't care. He never goes to practice
or my games.

4/G

Student Request For Counseling
with Mrs. Lampert

May I Please Talk To You About…

My step dad when he comes
over my mom starts being
mean to me.

5/G

I Whant to talk to you
about is my mom tells me to
do it this way but my mom
tell me to do another way
and if I don't do it my mom
way she hit me rllay hard
and if I don't do mis. ▓▓▓▓
way I mith get a F on my
report card

3/G

t.m
#2 Beacuse kids keep on Bodering me
and teasing me, and every kid Fight
with me beacuse of nothing. and it
dosen't matter in what table they
change me They will still be Fighting
with me and teasing me. And my
dad almost always Screams at me or
my sister when we do something wrong
and he always gets mad. That is why
im #2 and what makes me hoppy
is that my mom, dad and little sisters
will always be with me even though my
mom and my dad works. That is why im
#2 To Ms. Lamber My Favorite Trust
counceler. ♥

5/G

STUDENT REQUEST FOR COUNSELING

MAY I PLEASE TALK TO YOU ABOUT...

I want to talk about
my family and feelings.   5/G

STUDENT REQUEST FOR COUNSELING

MAY I PLEASE TALK TO YOU ABOUT...

My uncle had go hit by a truck and

I can not forget about it can you

help me and I just need somewhere to take

4/B

STUDENT REQUEST FOR COUNSELING

MAY I PLEASE TALK TO YOU ABOUT...

Some of the problems I'm

going through at home and

at school.

4/G

1/10

STUDENT REQUEST FOR COUNSELING

MAY I PLEASE TALK TO YOU ABOUT...

me and my dad have

problems.

4/B

STUDENT REQUEST FOR COUNSELING

MAY I PLEASE TALK TO YOU ABOUT...

My mom she said that when she
was 16 she ruend her Life that
mean she Dosent want me. please Help M

4/G

STUDENT REQUEST FOR COUNSELING

MAY I PLEASE TALK TO YOU ABOUT...

I need to talk to you
about my parents.

4/G

STUDENT REQUEST FOR COUNSELING

MAY I PLEASE TALK TO YOU ABOUT...

Mrs. Lamper my mom think's
that the problem in my house because
of me know, I want to go with my Dad

5/G

Student Request For Counseling
with Mrs. Lampert

May I Please Talk To You About…

I had the worst Tuesday in my life. I almost
broke my jaw yesterday, I felt like I was going
to throw up (and still do) We had the biggest fight ever…

5/G

Student Request For Counseling
with Mrs. Lampert

May I Please Talk To You About…

MY parents ~~Devorsing~~ Devorcing

3/G

Student Request For Counseling
with Mrs. Lampert

May I Please Talk To You About…

I have promblems with
my dad.

4/G

Student Request For Counseling
with Mrs. Lampert

May I Please Talk To You About…

About that my stepmom is going
to have a baby 3 then I don't know
because when my dad told me I cryed! more
4/G

Student Request For Counseling
with Mrs. Lampert

May I Please Talk To You About…

About my problems in my house
please don't don't call me
ask for me in school
4/G

Student Request For Counseling
with Mrs. Lampert

May I Please Talk To You About…

familly and bully
5/B

Student Request For Counseling
with Mrs. Lampert

May I Please Talk To You About…

Evrt time I tell My Mom Somthing She

Oant Belive me and gets mad me.

3/B

Student Request For Counseling
with Mrs. Lampert

May I Please Talk To You About…

My mom is about to have

surgery what do I do?

3/G

Student Request For Counseling
with Mrs. Lampert

May I Please Talk To You About…

I need to talk to you about

my mom I feel weird.   5/B

Student Request For Counseling
with Mrs. Lampert

May I Please Talk To You About...

Urgent My parents are pushing
me too much to be good ~~please~~ please   4/B
help me

My parents never respect me and when
I asked them to do something that   5/G
has to do with me they don't listen
to   me.

Dear, Ms.Lamperte

I want to talk about what
I hate about my house.   3/G

(my mom understood)
(everything.

"Thank
You
so much

Student Request For Counseling
with Mrs. Lampert

May I Please Talk To You About...

Mrs. Lampert, everything went great
when I talked to my mom
about the talk we had!

Student Request For Counseling
with Mrs. Lampert

May I Please Talk To You About…

My dad I have'int sean my dad sins crismis, I really miss my dad My he-y's I dad has a girlfriend she is the won that can't see my dad and my dad descn to her.

3/G

Student Request For Counseling
with Mrs. Lampert

May I Please Talk To You About…

my dad and me and my whole family.

5/G

Student Request For Counseling
with Mrs. Lampert

May I Please Talk To You About…

wat my father Did to my family. 4/G

97

I want to talk about
how my mom's cosin
is alaays huging
my sister that
is Biger than me
And I fell like
~~she~~ he Dose not ₃/ɢ
love me.

STUDENT REQUEST FOR COUNSELING

MAY I PLEASE TALK TO YOU ABOUT...

I got more prombl at
My hoos and I very very
need to see you.
5/ɢ

Student Request For Counseling
with Mrs. Lampert

May I Please Talk To You About…

My mom is sick so I am reaLy Sad can we tak about this 3/G

Student Request For Counseling
with Mrs. Lampert

May I Please Talk To You About…

my homesick promble 3/G

Student Request For Counseling
with Mrs. Lampert

May I Please Talk To You About…

I am Jest having a hard time at home

3/G

Dear, Dad

I wanted to send you this leter because I dont want to say it in your face because I'm scared. Did you enjoy ██████████? Did you breakup with ████? it kind shows we don't see much of her anymore? I know I see you often but I wish you and mom were together I know it will not happen but it gets sad some times. Oaky remember when I was crying and ████ was talking to me it was about you I hate it when you leave in the weekends we are with you cant you you come other time I love ~~to~~ you I just cant tell you this in your face,

4/G

* 4th grade girl writes a letter to her father expressing her feelings about divorce

Student Request For Counseling
with Mrs. Lampert

May I Please Talk To You About…

MY fami∂ in MY house how they treat me too

4/B

Student Request For Counseling
with Mrs. Lampert

May I Please Talk To You About…

My Dad and mom are Fighting with me because I told her my (shoes) (hurt) shouse hoort my feet. and she start screaming at me.

3/G

Dear Mrs. Lamper I would like to talk to you about my mom and my aunt and I wanna let it go but I can7.

3/G

Dear Mrs. Lampert

Last year I was the second smartest boy in the whole class. And everybody is in my class again this year. I have a baby brother and he is five months old. And I have a responsability and have to keep everything in my mind. I am very sick so it's hard for me to do all that.

4/G

Dear Dad

I want to know how are you doing I got good grades in my report card. Did you stop drinking or smoking? Did cough go away I feel Sad past the days II miss you very much! Why hadn't you called me. I call you on Ybirthday at work ████ miss you he said where's Daddy. When will you come home?

4/B

A Talk with my dad sounded mischiviosly bad when he said it was good, Makes me mad

3/G

Student Request For Counseling
with Mrs. Lampert

May I Please Talk To You About…

My Dad he hasn't called, and he
said he would call about the
first day, but he didn't   4/B

I
same boy
1 year apart

Student Request For Counseling
with Mrs. Lampert

May I Please Talk To You About…

me having trouble with my father
and to see if I should call him
since he hasn't called me   5/B

Mrs. Lamperd

Dear mrs. lamperd my life has been
hard because my dad moved out
of the house, my Tia moved to █████
my dog died, and my grandma died.

4/G

Chapter 7

Death

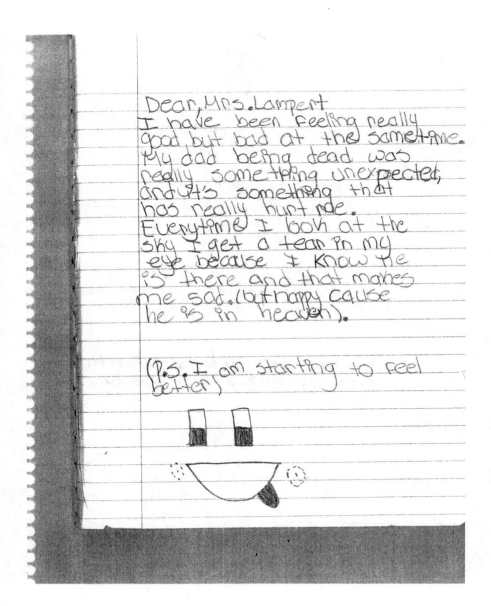

Dear, Mrs. Lampert
I have been feeling really
good, but bad at the sametime.
My dad being dead was
really something unexpected,
and it's something that
has really hurt me.
Everytime I look at the
sky I get a tear in my
eye because I know he
is there and that makes
me sad. (but happy cause
he is in heaven).

(P.S. I am starting to feel
better)

Student Request For Counseling
with Mrs. Lampert

May I Please Talk To You About…

I Fell Sad Cause my mon died.   3/G

May I Please Talk To You About…

I am Sad because my Grampa died I am very sad.   3/G

My Grandma died last Month I can't stop thinking of it how do you stop it.
                                         4/G

May I Please Talk To You About…

Sometimes when I think about my grandma I cry how do i get through it   5/G

when my mom die I was so sad
that I (thought) shot This was my falut
That she die I fult so mad I cold
beck the wall.
(break)

5/B

Student Request For Counseling
with Mrs. Lampert

May I Please Talk To You About...   4/G

My grandpa my granpa died about
2 years ago & I think of him every night
& cry but hold my tears when people sleep over and I dont know how
To stop.

STUDENT REQUEST FOR COUNSELING

MAY I PLEASE TALK TO YOU ABOUT...

My Grandfather because he is
dying from cancer   5/G

Dear Mrs. Lampert,
I want to know can I talk to you about my dad's death. I feel better a little. I am going to see him today at his grave. What should I tell him? Why I didn't go for Father's day. So I'll say happy Father's day. I want to talk to you about how my feelings got better.

P.S. Next time you call me can you call my brother too!

4/6

I love my dog but she is dead

STUDENT REQUEST FOR COUNSELING

MAY I PLEASE TALK TO YOU ABOUT...

One of my family dieing
Emergency   5/G

Student Request For Counseling
with Mrs. Lampert

May I Please Talk To You About...

My grandfather dyed and my Great Uncle ▮▮▮ is in the hospital   3/G
and I miss them very so.

Student Request For Counseling
with Mrs. Lampert

May I Please Talk To You About...   3/G

Mine Bird die and I miss him

STUDENT REQUEST FOR COUNSELING

MAY I PLEASE TALK TO YOU ABOUT...

The baby death It is major
important P.S. I have the   4/G
pictures

STUDENT REQUEST FOR COUNSELING

MAY I PLEASE TALK TO YOU ABOUT...

My Grandpa died a week ago   4/G

STUDENT REQUEST FOR COUNSELING

MAY I PLEASE TALK TO YOU ABOUT...   4/G

I want to talk to you about my friend
that died because he was sick and he stayed
in the hospital for 1year.

Dear   ,

I love you I'm
glad to come see
you. I'm geting good
grades and I'm and
the fifth grade.
I feel sad that you
is going to die. I wil
miss you want you
die. My family will
~~feel~~ feel sad.

Love.   5/G

When my mom die I wished I can
go back in time so I can stop it
Be for its to late So I don't missise
her That is my Words so now you
Know how I feel.

5/B

STUDENT REQUEST FOR COUNSELING

MAY I PLEASE TALK TO YOU ABOUT...

I want to talk about My Aunt who
got in a car accident and died and my step
Grandfather who died of a tumor.

5/G

STUDENT REQUEST FOR COUNSELING

MAY I PLEASE TALK TO YOU ABOUT...

Please talk to you about
death I need to
talk can you get me after Pe

5/B

STUDENT REQUEST FOR COUNSELING

MAY I PLEASE TALK TO YOU ABOUT...

Mrs Lamper my aunt had a baby but she lost it they didn't let her see the baby because the baby was in piece I am very sa

5/G

well my grand mother died and my grand father won't stop cry ing and my daddy has been mad lately and my dog ████ had a tomer with cancer and also had her life of death.

3/G

STUDENT REQUEST FOR COUNSELING

MAY I PLEASE TALK TO YOU ABOUT...

My Grandfather died

4/G

I would like to
tack in my group
of grils. Is did some
one has problems
at home or if some
one died and you
can not get over it.

4/G

STUDENT REQUEST FOR COUNSELING

MAY I PLEASE TALK TO YOU ABOUT...

ABout my ~~Be~~ mom bady sister
who ~~Be~~ die

4/G

STUDENT REQUEST FOR COUNSELING

MAY I PLEASE TALK TO YOU ABOUT...

MY PaBUM is MY pets aer keP
baiYing (dying)

1st grade boy

STUDENT REQUEST FOR COUNSELING

MAY I PLEASE TALK TO YOU ABOUT...

My dad Bin Being dead And my leter is
rely.

5/G

STUDENT REQUEST FOR COUNSELING

MAY I PLEASE TALK TO YOU ABOUT...

Someone who died in my
Family.

3/G

STUDENT REQUEST FOR COUNSELING

MAY I PLEASE TALK TO YOU ABOUT...

My Godfather that died and I
miss him very much.

4/G

dear mom i feel sad that you are
not here with me and i feel very
mad because you where the that
made me happy but i still know that
you are still in my heart but i still
wish that you where here with me. may
god bless you.   5/G

---

my topic
yesterDay I thought about my
DaD and I said to my self
I wish I was with my
DaD right Before He DieD so
I could have Htped Him get   5/B
the Heart act piLL and everything
would Be aL Right

When I had my (hurt) Mom I fult
like nobody can haunt me but wan
my Mom die I promes I will go to   5/B
chirch for my mom.

When my mom die I wished I can go back in time so I can stop it Be for its to late So I don't missise her That is my Words so now you Know how I feel.

3/G

It Seemslike

It seemslike someone comes and says that
ur not going to see him again. Until you die
at's when you'll see him It seem'like I said
s. But I didn't say it. He could of told me that
e was going and I won't see you again. I won't
say good-bye but I didn't and I will bame.my-
elf for this.

H/G

wow I hade The mast Terridle
Day of my life my ant Just
Died and I feel Bade in the
in side of me but I
rialy Dont know what to think
in the out sid of me I know
that once someone diase they
don't come Back But it's
hard for me toforget allabout
it I hade this ixpircns once
But I Dont want I again
Because it feels terrible.
I know that alot of people
has ixperensted This like
parrents. But Im small I
only eleven. I don't want
to be a sade man when I
grow up. and that is why
I wanted to tell you this
all of you expesholy mrs Lampert
Thank you all for helping me
with my Problems

4/3

*Relates this death
experience to the death
of his twin brother, age 4.*

I feel very bad that my mother is not here with me. She was very kind my father told me. My dad told me that he can Still here her voice in the hospital. I wish She was back with me in my house. And I think she had a soft voice. My dad Says that She is still in my heart. And I think he is right her sprite may go on but I will Still miss her no matter what. I wounder if She misses me. But I hope God will take care of her in heaven. 6/4

Chapter 8

Siblings

Mindi Lampert, MS, LMHC

Student Request For Counseling
with Mrs. Lampert

May I Please Talk To You About…

Just wanted to talk about my — 5/G
sister and its hard for me
its about that shes pregnat and shes broke up
with her
boy friend

I am starntin to think
I do hate my brother woth
do I do
3/G

May I Please Talk To You About…

Sometimes nobody never wants
to talk to me and my brothers
and sister won't even talk to me 3/G

Student Request For Counseling
with Mrs. Lampert

May I Please Talk To You About...

3/G

My brother is always hurting. he calls me names
and he bosses me around and he also hurts me
he pushes me and hits and i don't like it.

my brother is always mean
to me and he makes me
feel bad and he always calles
me names and he is always
mean to me

3/G

Student Request For Counseling
with Mrs. Lampert

May I Please Talk To You About…

I'm having a promblem that me   4/G
and My sister ████████ are having a
fight against whos the best of my mom.

Student Request For Counseling
with Mrs. Lampert

May I Please Talk To You About…

my sister dose not treet me   3/G
good. Shes meen to me.

Mrs.lampern

I am sad that my brother
is going to (colege) what do I do
I will miss him.
                                    4/B

Student Request For Counseling
with Mrs. Lampert

May I Please Talk To You About…

Dear Ms. Lampert my sister always has 4/G
to insult me every day. whenever my mom try's to
stop her she keeps on going and going

Student Request For Counseling
with Mrs. Lampert

May I Please Talk To You About…

that my sister always says
that I don't love her and 4/G
calls me the worst sister ever.

Student Request For Counseling
with Mrs. Lampert

May I Please Talk To You About…

My sister My sister is sick
she threw up and she just
came out of the hospital I'm worried 2/B

Mindi Lampert, MS, LMHC

STUDENT REQUEST FOR COUNSELING

MAY I PLEASE TALK TO YOU ABOUT...

if a cad help you and
if you cud help do things   2/G
to th tell my drother to stop messing
NAME with me.   GRADE/ROOM

My sister is 14 and
she tell me names
like stupid and I really
think im stupid   3/B

Student Request For Counseling
with Mrs. Lampert

May I Please Talk To You About...

my sister ran away
agnia   5/G

126

Chapter 9

Fear

I just have had my
house burned down
and I'm stressed
out. And worried something
esle bad going to hope.

4/G

STUDENT REQUEST FOR COUNSELING

MAY I PLEASE TALK TO YOU ABOUT...

Dear MS. lampert   I want to talk
with   about my Mom and dad
I am scared of the fight!? P.S Bring   4/G

STUDENT REQUEST FOR COUNSELING

MAY I PLEASE TALK TO YOU ABOUT...

Dear, Mrs. Lampert Iam So scared becouse
the war And I Need to talk to
a Grown up about it. P.S= bring   4/G

STUDENT REQUEST FOR COUNSELING

MAY I PLEASE TALK TO YOU ABOUT...

Something important and I'm
scared if something will
go rong. It is about My mom. 4/6

It's that my mom wants to
have a baby and I'm scared
that something might go rong
if she have it becouse she is 42. 5/6

Student Request For Counseling
with Mrs. Lampert

May I Please Talk To You About...

My Groma becous
she has canser. 3/G

Student Request For Counseling
with Mrs. Lampert

May I Please Talk To You About…

I have a friend who Hit's me
all the time and I am to scare   4/G
to tehere to stop she's not here enymore but
                                    She's.
                                    coming
                                    back.

Student Request For Counseling
with Mrs. Lampert

May I Please Talk To You About…

Mrs. Lampect I am scared   3/G
and I'm sleeping with my parents
and I'm scared of people telling me scary
                                    Stuff.
                                    I don't
                                    know
                                    what
                                    to do

Chapter 10

Anger

STUDENT REQUEST FOR COUNSELING

MAY I PLEASE TALK TO YOU ABOUT...

I try to cut my self with a stepol but I think about it 5/G
(staple)

Dear Ms. Lampard,

Can you help me get over my anger and nervouleness. I dont know why everytime I come to school I grab my book bag and dont like to follow the rules. I dont like to follow directions and I'm bad at spelling. Can you give me a test for exampe. If your teacher is giving a direction the answers I willpick will be play a game and pass letters.

4/B

STUDENT REQUEST FOR COUNSELING

MAY I PLEASE TALK TO YOU ABOUT...

About my dad and anger.

4/B

? not signed
probably about
a grade

my mom is going
to Kill me!!!

my mom is going to
Kill me!!!
I'm sorry mom!!!
I'm sorry mom! !!
I'm dead

I'm dead
I do want a better
education! It's hard
to swith my feelings
in one da... t'm s...

Student Request For Counseling
with Mrs. Lampert

May I Please Talk To You About…

how can I conntroll my Actions
if somebody is bothering me.   3/B

Student Request For Counseling
with Mrs. Lampert

May I Please Talk To You About…

a kid in my class he is all ways bothering
me and it is geting on nerves   3/B

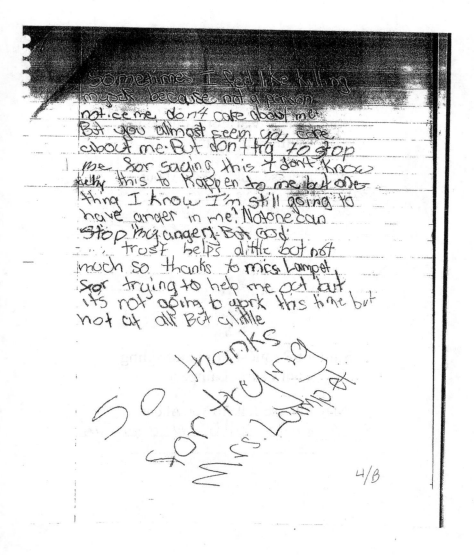

Sometimes I feel like killing mysdf, because not a person notice me, don't care about me. But you allmost seem you care about me. But don't try to stop me for saging this I don't know telly this to happen to me but one thing I know I'm still going to have anger in me? Noone can stop my anger. But God. trust helps a little but not much so thanks to mics Lampet for trying to help me got but it's not going to work this time but not at all But a little

So thanks for trying Mrs. Lampet

4/B

Student Request For Counseling
with Mrs. Lampert

May I Please Talk To You About…

Some one who get me mad.
I would want to talk to you to
help me talk about his person

3/G

Student Request For Counseling
with Mrs. Lampert

May I Please Talk To You About…

I need help with my angel isues.

4/B

Student Request For Counseling
with Mrs. Lampert

May I Please Talk To You About…

~~When~~ All the anger in me that I
want to take out

4/G

Student Request For Counseling
with Mrs. Lampert

May I Please Talk To You About…

I need to talk About a
Person in my class room   3/B
I try to Be nise to he makes me mad

May I Please Talk To You About…

Anger ISSUSes

3/B

Chapter 11

Domestic Violence

STUDENT REQUEST FOR COUNSELING

MAY I PLEASE TALK TO YOU ABOUT...

My mom and my dad are fighting and my dad was about to hit my mom

Please help me 4/G

STUDENT REQUEST FOR COUNSELING

MAY I PLEASE TALK TO YOU ABOUT...

my prensent hit each other and now there getting a devordest and my sad I don't know how to handly it

4/G

STUDENT REQUEST FOR COUNSELING

MAY I PLEASE TALK TO YOU ABOUT...

My uncle he fights alot with my ant once he send her to the Hospital.

4/G

STUDENT REQUEST FOR COUNSELING

To: Mrs. Lampert

MAY I PLEASE TALK TO YOU ABOUT...

My mom had a fight last night with my step Dad, and he try to break her head. 5/G

(Break her head)

STUDENT REQUEST FOR COUNSELING

MAY I PLEASE TALK TO YOU ABOUT...

My Brother try to hit him for my mom. 5/G

STUDENT REQUEST FOR COUNSELING

MAY I PLEASE TALK TO YOU ABOUT...

My Step Dad try to hit my mom yesterday. 3/G

Student Request For Counseling
with Mrs. Lampert

May I Please Talk To You About…

a problem that happened yesterday. It was about
my parents getting mad at each other and a hit ocurred to
Me.   5/B

MAY I PLEASE TALK TO YOU ABOUT…

I need to talk about family
violence and about mom
& and dad problem in family 4/G

The thing thapped a by
time ago

last year my mom was
bring some family my dad
like that family because we
get — food when my dad won't
to talk to my mom and when
My parnet was talk in the
bathroom when my dad came
out my mom got hat on
the eye but
My dad was not drunk   4/G

Chapter 12

Parents in Jail

&

Police Issues

Dear Ms. lampert I have bad news my
dad is geting out of jail in May I really not
happy and my grandmom is not happy at all but
She is doing find and my anty has to
go back to the hastipital for her heart I hope
She feels better and head hurts Because my little
Cousin stabed me in my head. But I'm feeling
a little better.

love ███

p.s And My Self of steam is lower ☹

— — — — — — — — — 3/G

MS. LamPer I Saw my Dad 3/G
yesterday and I need to tell
you how it went.
I need to see you ~~today~~ today
Can you call the class room
to send me after the meeting.

143

Student Request For Counseling
with Mrs. Lampert

May I Please Talk To You About...

my Parents are getting   5/G
me scared of all the
Places there takina me like Police
                                    Station

My momand steped Dad are
in Jail

4/G

STUDENT REQUEST FOR COUNSELING

MAY I PLEASE TALK TO YOU ABOUT...

My Dad did Something Bad
that My Family Started to 5/G
Cry.

144

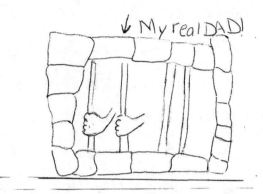

↓ My real DAD!

4/G

at

I need to talk to you about I have
home problems. I have problem like when my
stepdad goes to jail

4/G

a Realy DaD when my DaD got locked
up   I was Just Born and
it heat's me   when I see
a girl that's wiht   her DaD at the moives
our at the Sore and it heart me
to say all. Thieis Stuff But I
know if I Say it in ████ Grop
I know they would help me.
That's how I Fell all the
Time

4/6

Papi,

    I don't like what you do but who you are which is my father is what I like. I don't like what you did to us o feel bad that you're in jail and all and I'm sad that I don't live with you and mami but, maybe you two are learning your lesson for the horrible life you put me and my family through. I don't hate you I love you with all my heart. I just don't understand why you did it. I feel hurt that you and mami never got along. Tell me how you are going to change and why you are going to change. And, papi please tell me the truth. I love a lot remember the reason I'm writing you this letter is because I want to know the truth. Not that I hate you because I really love you. Sincerly,

5/G

Chapter 13

Alcohol & Drug
Use by Family

The first time that my dad had a problem in the family by getting drunk was when I was 4 yrs old. My dad and mom were arguing then when he went outside my mom locked the door and my dad had to sleep in his blue ████, when that happened I felt very scared.

B/4th

STUDENT REQUEST FOR COUNSELING

MAY I PLEASE TALK TO YOU ABOUT...

My dad that happen in Halloween because he was drink and fall down.

G/5th

STUDENT REQUEST FOR COUNSELING

MAY I PLEASE TALK TO YOU ABOUT...

My @ grandma is Dieing and My dad wont stop Drinking

G/5th

STUDENT REQUEST FOR COUNSELING

MAY I PLEASE TALK TO YOU ABOUT...

May I please talk with you anytime.
Possible Thank You Still kind about drugs
and anger also friends.   B/4th

Student Request For Counseling
with Mrs. Lampert

May I Please Talk To You About...

My sister wants to drink beer
and she is getting many   G/5th
collage applications and she might ruin her life.

STUDENT REQUEST FOR COUNSELING

MAY I PLEASE TALK TO YOU ABOUT...

My dad Drugs

B/4th

What Happened? <u>a boy in my class</u>

<u>is telling me that is brother is getting</u>

<u>drunk, he is also telling me that</u>

<u>he saw cocaine and sex he is</u>

<u>always telling me lets do this</u>

<u>It makes me feet unconftible</u>

<u>and ~~sed~~ wearyed. He ^{telling} igeep me that</u>

(since)
<u>Sings friday. He told me not to tell</u>

<u>because hell go to jail. He also</u>

is
drinks with him. Ones time he ~~told~~
mealways looking at me and drawing
privets

G/4th

Student Request For Counseling
with Mrs. Lampert

May I Please Talk To You About…

I want to know that I want to talk about my mom and my stepFather smoke alot and she Does Drugs. Please I wanna talk to you.

3/G

Student Request For Counseling
with Mrs. Lampert

May I Please Talk To You About…

well my mom started drinking again and other stuff. 3/G

STUDENT REQUEST FOR COUNSELING

MAY I PLEASE TALK TO YOU ABOUT...

My aunt and uncle my DaD
AND Uncle came Drunk and
my uncle gotin a fight with my aunt

sorry I couldn't make it to drop

G/5th

STUDENT REQUEST FOR COUNSELING

MAY I PLEASE TALK TO YOU ABOUT...

Hello miss Lamper
How are you doing will
I am doing great Because my

dad is not drinking (Eny more)

G/3rd

Dear Mrs. Lampert,

5/G

In New years eve I felt terrible.
I never get to enjoy my New Years
because I always feel sad its just
that like my dad he gets drunk and
he hurts my feelings really
bad. I don't want to say everything
because its very long I need
advice. Can you please talk to
me. I need to talk to you fast.

Chapter 14

Physical Abuse

Student Request For Counseling
with Mrs. Lampert

May I Please Talk To You About…

my Dad miss treating my mom on the phone and face to face. and I am scarred that he going to hit her.

4/B

Student Request For Counseling
with Mrs. Lampert

May I Please Talk To You About…

my Dab puch me wednesday

(Punch)

4/G

Student Request For Counseling
with Mrs. Lampert

May I Please Talk To You About…

3/B

MY Dad Hit ME after MY surgery of my heart.

Student Request For Counseling
with Mrs. Lampert

May I Please Talk To You About…

3/13

My step father choking my Broth
er out of the room because my
Brother did not want to get out of the room

Student Request For Counseling
with Mrs. Lampert

May I Please Talk To You About…

my grandfather hit my
sisters he even asotd my
sisters. (assaulted)

3/8

Student Request For Counseling
with Mrs. Lampert

May I Please Talk To You About…

thatmkmom trt tok'llmkdad and
She breakstufwhen Shesmad anti hate
whenshecrxs Soihelphen 3/B

[That my mom try to kill my dad and
she break stuff when she's mad and i hate
when she cries so i help her.]

Student Request For Counseling
with Mrs. Lampert

3/B

May I Please Talk To You About…

Could I talk about my parents
hitting me when they are angry

Chapter 15

Sexual Abuse

Student Request For Counseling
with Mrs. Lampert

May I Please Talk To You About…

I dont Feel good um yesterday
Somting happen and I would
like to talk to You

3/G

He made me put my
mouth in IS Dick.

3/G

Student Request For Counseling
with Mrs. Lampert

May I Please Talk To You About…

4/G

Somting that happend to me
at my complex and I realy want violate
to talk to you a boy was trying to violate me

when I talked about
the sexual Abuse I felt
happier when I talked
About it because I was
Able to take that out
of My feeling and I
like my ███████ counseling
Group because we hear
to each other and we
listend and another
thing ~~that~~ I went to
say is that I don't
like my ~~grandma~~
foster mom because
she screams me alot
and to do alot of
jobs so I don't
like the way she
treats me but I
like the Group Ms.
LampERt and another
feeling that is
hearting my feeling
that I do not want
to be with this phoster
mom and I prefer
to live with my
Grandma because
she aint mean like the Group
My ~~fost~~ foste mom
was nice to share with ~~you~~

4/G

Chapter 16

Friendship

██████ is Bieng
A bully and I'm trying
to Fitt ih whith my
Freinds and he is
Saing in anberasing
thinas a bout me
and he wont stop
can you help me? 3/6

Dear, Ms. Lampert

I am having friend
issues. Can you help me?
3/6

Student Request For Counseling
with Mrs. Lampert

May I Please Talk To You About…

███ CONVINCED my only FriENd to Not be my FriENd so How do v think people mAke FriENds? 4/B

Student Request For Counseling
with Mrs. Lampert

May I Please Talk To You About…

███ and ███ called me a "Bich" on FaceBook. 5/G

Student Request For Counseling
with Mrs. Lampert

May I Please Talk To You About…

a kid are ding Mean to me he leme pleas 3/G

Student Request For Counseling
with Mrs. Lampert

May I Please Talk To You About…

I have problems what do we do. P.s- with people they think They know me. but they don't. 5/G

Student Request For Counseling
with Mrs. Lampert

May I Please Talk To You About…

Something about my frenids About my freihals not likeing or play with me. 3/B

Student Request For Counseling
with Mrs. Lampert

May I Please Talk To You About…

Two boy that Like my but if I tell the other one that I don't Like him I'll breake his fealings 3/G

Student Request For Counseling
with Mrs. Lampert

May I Please Talk To You About...

Theres a girl that bothers
me but not me but the whole
class that have 43 students

4/G

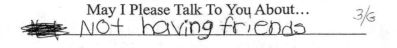

Student Request For Counseling
with Mrs. Lampert

May I Please Talk To You About...

My friend I me on Monday.
You got in to a fight. Call my
BFF

3/G

Student Request For Counseling
with Mrs. Lampert

May I Please Talk To You About...   3/G

NOt having friends

Student Request For Counseling
with Mrs. Lampert

May I Please Talk To You About…

MY friend Punch me At MY house
Punch me in The Stomach and
Threw a rock at me in my face.

3/B

Student Request For Counseling
with Mrs. Lampert

May I Please Talk To You About…

This girl in my class is mean to
me if I'm her friend and if she's
not my friend.

4/G

Student Request For Counseling
with Mrs. Lampert

May I Please Talk To You About…

friends with gossip about
MY

5/G

STUDENT REQUEST FOR COUNSELING

MAY I PLEASE TALK TO YOU ABOUT...

my friend has many qualities that I really don't like should I still be friends with her? G/4th

Student Request For Counseling
with Mrs. Lampert

May I Please Talk To You About...

My Fr Friend told my best Friend so she is mad at me. 4/6

Student Request For Counseling
with Mrs. Lampert

May I Please Talk To You About...

I fight I had with my friend. I NEED YOUR HELP PLEASE! 5/6

Student Request For Counseling
with Mrs. Lampert

May I Please Talk To You About…

~~My best friend~~ My Best friend is my
worst enemey now 🚗 what should I Do.   3/G

Student Request For Counseling
with Mrs. Lampert

May I Please Talk To You About…   5/G

My best friend stop being my friend.   –

Student Request For Counseling
with Mrs. Lampert

May I Please Talk To You About…

My Friend move and I want 3/G
to no want can I do to get over
it. And how can I get my best friend back

Student Request For Counseling
with Mrs. Lampert

May I Please Talk To You About...

My friends ~~so~~ like we are
friends and then we are
not.   3/6

Student Request For Counseling
with Mrs. Lampert

May I Please Talk To You About...   3/6

In class ~~so~~ people treat me bad. But
I treat them good. They always bother me.
Also when ever we do parnter work they just
look at
my work
and copy
it.

I am new and I am afraid to
talk to pepole. I am have ing
problems make ing friends. 3/6

Student Request For Counseling
with Mrs. Lampert

May I Please Talk To You About…

There is a girl I like and
I dont knows if she like
me   3/B

Student Request For Counseling
with Mrs. Lampert

May I Please Talk To You About… 3/G

Theres a gie who is
crazy to me but I cant
handle him He's in my class.

Student Request For Counseling
with Mrs. Lampert

May I Please Talk To You About…

Cause   thats in my class
                is   mean to me cause she   4/G
thinks she controls my life.

Chapter 17

Sexuality
&
Gender Issues

STUDENT REQUEST FOR COUNSELING

MAY I PLEASE TALK TO YOU ABOUT...

I almost killed myself
Last night I need to talk
about that

5/G

STUDENT REQUEST FOR COUNSELING

MAY I PLEASE TALK TO YOU ABOUT...

my sexcality

4/B

Student Request For Counseling
with Mrs. Lampert

May I Please Talk To You About...

our Friend is Asking us a Question
bout turning Bysexsual.

5/G

176

Chapter 18

Uncategorized Issues

Student Request For Counseling
with Mrs. Lampert

May I Please Talk To You About…

Lying to my parents and teachers

5/G

STUDENT REQUEST FOR COUNSELING

MAY I PLEASE TALK TO YOU ABOUT…

My teacher complains that I talk to much can you help me?

4/G

STUDENT REQUEST FOR COUNSELING

MAY I PLEASE TALK TO YOU ABOUT…

I want to be someone special when I grow up & how can I start a beautician when

5/G

HOW I FEEL TO BE IN A GANG

Let me give you some lesson of how I feel to be in a gang. I feel cool, I also don't feel scare or friend, I feel happy to be in a gang and I feel like being thear all my life. And never get out. And I don't feel scare beacuse I am brave, but when I hard this girl die, I felt a litte l sick. But it scool being in thear, we have to fun and eat what we want to eat, some of my friend do drugs but I don't care, but I know I will never take a drug, I am so happy with my friends I forget about proubles in my family when I am with them, I also have fun we get to be in our tree hose and talk and Then go to walk and pant in the walls. And thats my lessons of how I feel to be in a gang.

5/G

STUDENT REQUEST FOR COUNSELING

MAY I PLEASE TALK TO YOU ABOUT...

I hecd to toK to you oK
and I heed to tel Yoy Suchg
So Kmh aht pikme up

Translation:

1st grade/G

I need to talk to you OK
and I need to tell you something
so come and pick me up

Student Request For Counseling
with Mrs. Lampert

May I Please Talk To You About...

My jeasly

5/G

I feel very streessted I feel like if I have a spirit in me I dont feel good sece this morning.

4/B

I'm mad, sad and not happy that my Dad smokes around me and my littal Brother.

4/B

Student Request For Counseling
with Mrs. Lampert

May I Please Talk To You About...

My teacher and other stuff, like My Grades and a problem with someone.

5/G

Student Request For Counseling
with Mrs. Lampert

May I Please Talk To You About... (problem)

hi, I Don't have a prompel
I just want to See you   4/G

Dear Ms. Lamper,
                    Thank
you for helping
me with my
Problems and I
won't forget
how good you
made me feel!   5/G

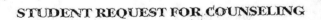

STUDENT REQUEST FOR COUNSELING

MAY I PLEASE TALK TO YOU ABOUT...

THank you   four   talking   with
me   about   my   problems   thank   5/G

Mrs Lampert

hi Mrs Lampert
I Love you for what
you did today and
that was good and
that is why I Love
you but at yas not
the only and you
are beautiful and so
good to be my
mother and I
would Love for
you to be my
mother and that
is why I Love
you because you are
my mother.

4/G

183

MS LamprE

You are The
most nices
Techer in
The world
me and
The hole
gorup Loves
you and You
are The Best
Thats why your
The nises hart
in a wor Lives.
and You Your
self PuT seed's
oF Love

3/G

Dear Ms. Lampard
Thank you so much for helping
me. Know i now that i can talk
to someone that won't
tell anyone. And i can trust
you.

From: Girl

class: 3rd grade

Chapter 19

Issues they cannot write…..

Student Request For Counseling
with Mrs. Lampert

May I Please Talk To You About...

Something that is in my mind that
I can't get out. It is bothering me
I cannot work very well.   3/G

STUDENT REQUEST FOR COUNSELING

MAY I PLEASE TALK TO YOU ABOUT...

Something I need to say bad only need one
minute   4/B

Student Request For Counseling
with Mrs. Lampert

May I Please Talk To You About...   4/G

Can't say out loud

Student Request For Counseling
with Mrs. Lampert

May I Please Talk To You About…

I need to talk about Why I was
not here and it is bothering
me alot and I think you need to know   4/G

STUDENT REQUEST FOR COUNSELING

MAY I PLEASE TALK TO YOU ABOUT…

Mrs I need to talk to you
about something very important   5/G
I can't write Down

Student Request For Counseling
with Mrs. Lampert

May I Please Talk To You About…

My life thatts happening to me   4/B

Student Request For Counseling
with Mrs. Lampert

May I Please Talk To You About…

I neeed to ~~mamke~~ talk with you I cant
write it so qlease I need to talk
to you

5/G

Student Request For Counseling
with Mrs. Lampert

May I Please Talk To You About…

@ heoll @ I have a lot
on my mine can I see you
some day

5/G

Student Request For Counseling
with Mrs. Lampert

May I Please Talk To You About…

private stuff ~~oot~~

5/G

Dear Ms Lampert,
　　I'm having some problems
at home If it's ok don't tell
my parents about this They
don't allow me to talk about
it, but I just need to get it
out of my system

5/G

STUDENT REQUEST FOR COUNSELING

MAY I PLEASE TALK TO YOU ABOUT...

I need to say I have
some problems.

4/G

Student Request For Counseling
with Mrs. Lampert

May I Please Talk To You About…

Pregnesy

3/G

I want to tall
you abut my
fillings becuse
school is
allmost out
and I want
to tall you
abut my
filling tomoro
Have a good
Day,

2/G

STUDENT REQUEST FOR COUNSELING

MAY I PLEASE TALK TO YOU ABOUT...

Something that's going though my mind

4/B
.112

Student Request For Counseling
with Mrs. Lampert

May I Please Talk To You About...

My attidude

5/G

Student Request For Counseling
with Mrs. Lampert

May I Please Talk To You About...

My Actions

4/G

STUDENT REQUEST FOR COUNSELING

MAY I PLEASE TALK TO YOU ABOUT...   4/G

My life

STUDENT REQUEST FOR COUNSELING

MAY I PLEASE TALK TO YOU ABOUT...

Today I have a bad day I just.
whent to see you. Today.
3/B

I wan't to talk to yau
because I am having flash
backs.
5/G

Dear mrs lampart

I wont to talk to you in private
because I'm having some problems
to keep my concentration. because
I keep thinking about no I'll get
a detrntion so I got a sitation
oh we got a rcd I got too
much tension. can you help me
3/G

Student Request For Counseling
with Mrs. Lampert

May I Please Talk To You About…

I HATE MY LIFE!
5/G